SOFT GEOGRAPHY

Soft geography

GILLIAN WIGMORE

Caitlin Press

Published by Caitlin Press
P.O. Box 219, Madeira Park BC von 2H0
www.caitlin-press.com

Author photo by Travis Sillence.
Cover design by Anna Comfort.

Caitlin Press acknowledges financial support from the Province of British Columbia through the British Columbia Arts Council, for its publishing activities.

BRITISH
COLUMBIA
ARTS COUNCIL
Supported by the Province of British Columbia

Library and Archives Canada Cataloguing in Publication

Wigmore, Gillian, 1976–
    Soft geography / Gillian Wigmore.

Poems.
ISBN 1-894759-23-0

    1. British Columbia--Poetry. I. Title.

PS8645.I34S63 2007   C811'.6   C2007-902530-7

for Jenni
1977–1998

RANGING

WORD OF MOUTH

VET'S DAUGHTER

THE AGATE HUNTERS

FALL AND BURN

ranging

MARSH

spent grasses bend to the train's wind
burnt to wisps by the autumn sun

a rustle in the marsh
a catch in your throat

after melt-off
bracken and loss

the sky the mountains
the marsh the sky

your insides cartwheel
you feel your actual size

APRIL

in the ice house
we fish the dark holes
for burbot and char
imagine them slow,
swimming the cold water
under miles of ice.

we give thanks to the lake
for fear of its wrath
and feed fish to our children
with warnings: black water
lulls the best of us, that being
those of us left.

april's cold nights leak
into blank blue mornings.
the fish under the ice circle
the hooks we bait
with sweet corn and shrimp –
suspicious even as they desire,
enticed by the sharp and the sweet
as we are lured by a lake
we know will kill us –
not when we want it to
and not once,
but ceaselessly.

the ice moves
through the winter like a bear
uncomfortable in its hibernation.
it groans in the night, cries,
grinds itself into itself
until it's gone – the water rises
late in the spring,
it rattles the rocks onshore
like bones hanging
from a cottonwood.
all winter we rest,
apprehensively. in april,
we watch the west for storms.

NAMELESS

call up the walls and depth
without saying *canyon* –
in canada, naming the natural
phenomena is overdone.
down deep where light,
moon or otherwise, can't get,
the water waits on nothing.
it's nameless, once it shucks
all that colonial stuff off.

beyond the feedlots
and the miles of busted fence
where mending rests
only in the minds
of dead settlers,
beyond the dirty stories
they tell in the bar
at the chinese place on main street,
beyond the glossy pictures
gone grey and wet in the rain,
beyond that and outside of town,
the crack in the arc of the earth,
the whole gouged-out line of it
says *river river river*
how rivers say it
with water.

unmarked creeks offend us less
if we never see them –
paths worn rough into cliffsides
greased with history
don't call candlefish to mind
held aloft like bright torches.
this one river
at work on the earth,
wears down the map
to blankness and pulp,
without pause,
without thought,
and nameless
without regret.

the car twisted, after its several rolls, so you had to crawl out
like a grub from the dirt, like a bear after winter,
like a naked, squinting being who humbly seeks the light.

the car was a tunnel, the sky too far up to reach.
with glass underfoot and stuff tossed willy nilly
all you saw was wreckage, no horizon to understand.
the car was a well. you stood at the bottom,
underwater looking up at the featureless sky.
cue the rain.

there is no way out of memory;
the car is a candy uneaten. the accident is the time
you almost choked but breathed again.
the glide and flight of the car from the roadside
is the addiction you never had to alcohol
and rum-soaked raisins, the chicken you meant to kill
so you could eat it and justify the eating of flesh –
you remember your own surprised eyes staring out
of a spiderwebbed windshield even though
you never saw it from that angle. you and the car,
you are sisters in ditches and wreckage.

the cave-in of your life can be traced
back to this moment – not the crash
nor the tumble, nor the wrapping
of your various scrapes with makeshift bandages,
but this deep hole of a second, looking up,
when your view offered no answers to your salvaging
and you asked yourself:
is that really up?
is this all that's left?
do I want out?

SMALL WONDER

once on the water we see more than we expect:
a depth of pure jellyfish below us
and gannets dropping like accidents
out of the hot winter sky

on land, wild goats bar our way to the outhouse
we begin asking ourselves and each other
is there another way? sharks bask offshore,
baracudas eat our lunch off the line

I incubate our few options, and brood and wonder
if twenty kilometres by water means more to you
than dinner, than my throbbing wrists
than the start of life we both guessed at
and missed, amazed all the while
by incandescence swirled from a paddle tip

there is more landscape inside the tent than out
more sandflies than bites on my arm
more sacrifices to make than either of us can count
and neither of us counts – we steam the mussels
in south island plonk, straight out of the silver bag
you feed me one off the fork

food offers no answers, but satisfies
the parts of us desiring. what we don't know
is greater than the darkening landscape
the strange hills behind us, our pot at our feet

we gather our heat in the space between us
and feed our unshaped fear
with fish still cold and twitching

> *There is more landscape inside this tent/ Than out*
> –Charles Lillard

TENT: NO SHELTER

when the wind is more real
than the earth, than the tent
than the whip and break
of waterproof fabric
in front of your face
where you lie face-up to a storm
of tremendous proportions
that hammers the mountaintop
and the face of the earth
where you lie wishing for light,
for just another morning
so the battering ends

a break

and then you hear it coming
ripping up the slope
to ram the tent broadside
flat across your chest
open eyes, closed eyes,
full bladder, tears
nothing matters but that sound
the wind
backing off the better
to pounce

when the tent is no shelter
when your legs are useless
from packing your useless home
twenty miles in a day
you lie down on volcanic rock
to wait for the weather
to have no persona,
no desire to shred you –
erosion is a horrible thought

the bones of the tent
wear holes through their sockets
the sleeves of man-made fabric
weaken and rip
and the wind when it lets up
lets only the tent up

you lie still until morning
not trusting the stillness,
the silence, the earth to be whole
when you unzip
when you outstretch
and rise into a scoured day
unrested and worn ragged

when the wind retreats
do you raise your arms in victory?
or do you pee weakly behind a bush –
weary, but obviously living?

TENT: SHAMELESS

at the top of the campground and the first we see
we set up with the wide front door facing north,
the entire bay laid out like dinner before us
we stay for days, try to make a home
in a windtunnel, on a hillock, neighbour to goats.

sitting on our rooftop, inhaling, exhaling
the bright water glints off our pack zips
your bootlaces stretch out

I say, *it's time to leave*
the sky is our moonroof

no leaving today, you say
I am your moonroof, and prove it

in the tent again we hear boats roar
in the harbour, vendors swear, couples pass
on their way to the washrooms – we hear
arguments, thunder, barking and drunken raving –
we lie on our mats, tangled in sleeping bags,
talking of sex, graphically, demonstratively,
sure in the privacy one millimeter
of man-made fabric offers us –
we whoop it up then emerge squinting
unabashed, ready to wash up and move on
we drop the tent
already dripping with heat

BUS DRIVING ACROSS AMERICA

bus driving across america you find your greater self
sweating, legs stuck to the vinyl of the seat.
the land is what's left you after the failure of every kind of
metaphor,

after you've digested the books and diner fare.
you could make a pass at the girl with charcoal hair, or not.
bus driving across america you find your greater self

and that should be enough, but isn't.
the grand canyon scours your insides blank:
the land is what's left after the failure of every kind of metaphor.

how hard could it be to wax poetic,
crack yourself open, so that the miles matter?
bus driving across america, your greater self finds you

weeping in the road glare
sick to death of billboards and desire:
the land is what's left after you fail to find a metaphor

great enough to encompass the great man you'll become.
so grand you're bursting, bus driving across america,
failing the metaphors, the land, all that's left you.

The land is what's left
after the failure
of every kind of metaphor.
–Pat Lowther

THE FISH GARBAGE

crows cycled and recycled
through the hazy mix of hot garbage and air thermals.
blue cellophane fish guts crawled with maggots,
dragonfly larvae attacked small fish in the bay,
and I walked, looking for used toilet paper and plastic cutlery
in the bushes. small birds hopped just metres ahead
peering back to see if I followed.

and yes, I followed, in dirty polyester pants and uniform,
I followed the ruby-throated and the piliated.
I ate at the dock hoping to spot mergansers, grandeur,
those who skitter then soar.
the boatlaunch garbage was the best spot:
it drew flies and stray dogs,
and eagles in pairs talon-scratched
the concrete looking for leftovers.

aware of my intrusion but indifferent
birds landed and fought for morsels –
gorged on spleen, spines,
eyeballs and offal heated to delicacy
by the weight of the sun.
black plastic degassed slowly
into the organs of crows and eagles,
from the bags in the back of my truck into my lungs.
I formed a dirty kinship with refuse eaters:
one I pined all summer for.

STELLAKO

swans on fraser lake beat the water, rising
enormous and unlikely, with hardly lift enough
to miss the highway overpass
black beaks streaming in the rain

WINTERLY

at midday the mountains across the valley
pulse in the light
while here it could be dusk

the car stutters to life but fails
the frost coats the inside of the windshield
on this side of the valley it's winter

sometimes I can't tell what is dreamed
and what is lived: frost bite on cheekbones
from breath-mist freezing, sunlight on bare skin

I trudge to work, winterly
stars fall flaming into the reservoir
when the elk block the pathways in the shade, I wait

the river falls green down
its long old riverbed toward flat land
and in the mountains the heat is sucked hard

into whomever
is so lucky
to receive

HOLDING

weren't waiting for the boat's wake
to hit the shore weren't waiting
for the sun to rise higher – it was evening
weren't waiting for the end of it
for night for morning for awakening
of any sort weren't waiting
I swear it
weren't waiting

still think of seals off our point
still think of whales and sea monsters
still think of legend even lying half-asleep
beside girls so shapely I could burst open or cry
weren't waiting to sleep or wake
wasn't crying

still no whales but there might be deeper down
still no wake no waves just water and evening
all still
dark drifting in like it was waiting
for its cue

and us all three still waiting to be famous
still waiting for death still waiting
for some great burst from the sun to tan us
more beautiful more young more praiseworthy
but its sunset now and just getting colder
weren't waiting for seals but we'd follow

if they guided us in off the rocks
bucking between wavelets
minding behind them to see if we
were head up
and holding

DARK LAKE

1
white floats mark ling lines
heavy-baited and lethal
down deep in dark water

onshore grey jays shark-attack crumbs
then hunt each other down

the undergrowth is overgrown

2
fog lingers late into morning
on an uninviting beach
strewn with wet logs and pits
where fires once burned
with no one gathered round

3
near the water the birds go still:

storm debris hangs from low branches
summer-thin cotton shirts
and condom wrappers

sodden paper and cigarette butts mar the shore
cedar fronds drip in the dirt

down the beach a parked truck
with doors yawned open, empty inside
its tires sunk rim-deep in sand

word of mouth

there was a party at someone's cabin, maybe it was christmas. he was drinking rye and cokes, chasing them with beer. it was the beer I tasted in his mouth when he pushed me against the inside frame of the ice hut. a two-by-two down my spine, the taste of him. he put his hands in the front of my black down jacket. the night outside crackled. the ice shifted and moaned like a pod of whales passing beneath us. when I looked up I could see fuzzy stars through the wavy plastic ceiling. he kissed my neck. my husband. his banged-up hands and badly cut blond hair – hair I'd cut while smoking a cigarette in the kitchen, the baby asleep on the bed.

I remember spinning in the blue-walled hut on the lake, the tarps sucking in and out with the wind. I started to cry and he gave up kissing me. he looked at my face, patted the puffy front of my jacket and went out the plywood door.

that night is clear in mind – the wind ripping across the lake, the rumble of the party onshore, the black bank of trees. I walked toward the lights in my felt packs, the snow squeaking underfoot. drunk. that's who I was. winter, year one.

BEACH FIRE

god, shorty, you got me fired right up –
six-foot sturgeon leaping from the lake
in the night, no less,
and the wind, fuck,
that wind whips up
and old grandma in her aluminum putt-putt be damned.

that's the life, hey shorty?
the jack pine and those cottonwood dropping their cotton –
the nights smell so sweet you're drunk on it.
the wind and the waves pounding,
I want to ride the water when it gets like that.
christ. I never knew a lake that wants to kill you so bad.

I learned to read water from drunks and blind men.
you know bob,
well, his brother used to boat down the river at night –
he knew every boulder, every rapid,
there are men like that, shorty.

do you remember those nights?
the fish licking the surface til it boiled
how we knew it would storm
that black sky, the wind building up in portage
and blasting us back to fort.
cheers to that.

the water's yellow with pollen after the weather
and it coats your legs.
ah, shorty, my sister's son went out in it.
I found his ball cap washed up at cottonwood beach.
I don't know if fish are worth it,
not even sturgeon.
I'm sick of waiting for relatives to wash up.
that fucking lake,
kids washing up with their bellies swollen,
young kids drunk and then dead.

but when the wind gets up, shorty,
we're out there anyway,
you can't help it.
you want to beat the water,
the boat slapping like a beaver tail
and you have to shout to get anything heard.
we're shouting anyway, shorty,
full of cotton and water and wind.

MAL DE GORGE AT THE MERCY OF WORD OF MOUTH
(this is a true story)

history's got this method of simplification
it's got to do with essay writing
where, inside the word *concise*
the story can be told completely:

over a hundred years ago in new caledonia the carrier
(taculli, dakelh, porteurs, depending on how you tell it)
they had a fight:
there was blood, hair, bodies, feet
(crushed berry baskets, crushed clover)
they were attacked

mal de gorge fled
(in thunderous sunshine)
he snatched his baby brother and little sister
and jumped in the river
(arrows in the current)
he swam away
from babies split and stuck on stakes to dry like salmon

(imagine the thock of rock and body meeting)
(imagine the quiet below the churning chopped-up water)

his brother rolled away
over stones (bumped
alongside trout and algae) away
from mal de gorge
his brown legs thrashing

history has a history of simplification
how can you write *horror* and expect it to mean anything?
and once on the other side of the river
where did he go?
this story doesn't say

the storms pass
they pummel and pass like a battle
and afterwards
grass grows eventually
(the bent stalks stand)

this is only a place and a story, after all
(but bless the people killed
the bruised landscape, the sky)
and god bless mal de gorge with a name like that
(a real-life-story person
drowned in imaginary detail)
at the mercy of word of mouth

Jim we been meeting here every other day for five years and I din't ever tell you this but I am so goddam bored I might take my own life.

Jim I like the coffee and yer a funny bastard but I hate this town. I din't ever live anywhere but here or five miles from here and it never got any better. Din't get worse but it din't ever get better, neither.

Lucy's hands are gimped now, Jim, and she can't sew, nor knit. She used ta do these sweaters that sold in tourist shops on Vancouver Island and all the guys I worked with were always askin me when she would knit one fer them. Her hands look like feet now.

When she talks she says, *Don, yer not the man I married. That guy'd get me tea without first askin. That guy bought me flowers and dug up my garden every spring. That guy din't ever complain.* When she talks I wanna plug my ears up, Jim, and I used ta love her.

Jim we been meeting here a long time and I wanna say it means a lot ta me that you make jokes and tell those stories like that one about the guy's wife gave him packs of Dad's cookies instead a sanwiches in his lunch and the one how you fooled em inta givin you early retirement. Jim I like yer laugh and that's a intimate thing ta say.

But Jim either I'm not coming ta this café anymore or I gotta think somethin up cause I'm about ta give up. I am. I hate my wife's voice and I'm sick about her hands and I wish I just had somethin ta give her or do for her, but all I got's this hour an a half every other day talkin with you and the other guys ta keep me from doin myself in, Jim.

You want more coffee?

34

Jim I'm gonna tell you a secret. I snuck Lucy's knitting case out of the spare room without her seeing it. I got it here. Jim you know how ta knit? Does June? Cause I got an idea Jim. I don't ever do nothin and I just sit with these damn thoughts and I think if I could knit like Lucy used ta, maybe she wouldn't miss it so much. I know that's a crazy idea, but if I could knit and purl up something ta give her, or somethin I could maybe sell or give ta the hospital like she used ta, maybe she'd come round ta me again. Whadya think? Your June knits, don't she? Can't June knit?

Thing is Jim I gotta do it here at the café and I need you on my side, alright? You're a funny guy Jim and if you start laughin, you know they all will too. So are you in? I'm goin ta start small, don't you worry. Maybe socks or somethin. Somethin I can fit under the table so it's not so 'parent what I'm doin. You in Jim? You think June'd mind? I got the needles right here.

Jim we both know what they say about you round town but yer a good guy Jim, real good and I'm glad ta know you. You can tell em I said that.

FRANCOIS

there is no harbour where we married –
just the straight stretch of rock and sand
they stood us on for photographs,
stiff in the cool air, goosebumps all over.
willow, yes, and that big hard lake
stretching out to either side
of a foreshortened horizon.
the sun lit the hills twice that afternoon,
and the lake stayed black.

no harbour, but the photos are beautiful.
by the end of the day my ringlets blew east, slightly
bobbing in the breeze, my sisters laughed with their hands
         on their mouths.

the wind picked up at the edges.
by nightfall the men pulled the boats far up the beach,
battened down the tarps.
all the fishing boats went home.
when they toasted the bride the barn lit up,
torched from within, by lightning.

GIFT HORSES

I keep the house and surrounding yard
not very well and not diligently
but with an eye on the neighbourhood
and an ear out for the children's voices
expert at testing the timbre of cries
you know: run, don't start running just yet

the victimhood of others cramps my style
pulls my even stitches awry
I didn't change my name, isn't that enough?
I buy whole grains
I relish my husband's attentions

who looks a gift horse down his long horse throat?
not I – the horse road is worn
and the horses are too many
a herd even, or a murder
they tromp the roses I didn't plant and never water

whose story is this, anyway?
a woman at the end of a movement
with no apron and few piercings
flour on her hands
stretchmarks, a degree

philosophies sail about like dust in sunshine
the neighbour's horse chews the top of the fence
and most days, nothing forward
nothing back
nothing gained
but the chop, chop of hacking it

TIN BOAT

the lake was wretched this spring and higher than ever before
I know because I swam in it
the boat was breaking I had to do something
I could hear a banging – bang bang on the beach
the water was in the trees
the trees were up to their hips in water
the waves were terrible
they'd sucked the beach rocks out
to make a hollow the boat rode down
then up
then crash onto the rocks

the baby was asleep in the cabin
I stepped away from the willows into the water
I climbed in thinking how stupid
I'll die tonight and no one will know
the baby will starve
we'll be a story they tell at family reunions
the cousins will shake their heads and sigh

the water was shocking cold and fierce
it pulled my flipflops from my feet
I fell in the hollow under water in the dark
the boat banged above me
I got my foot on a rock and held onto the tin
I banged with the waves against the boat
against the shore the stars coming into and out
of view through the water and throughout
I thought of the baby
I thought of her dad
I held onto the night then let go

deep in this lake is a river no one believes in
I felt its pull
I felt its greater cold in the cold deep lake
I felt it with one toe and kicked for africa
kicked god help me kicked
I heard the baby
I heard the fish I heard that bloody boat
bang bang the corner of that goddamn bay
I kicked the river in the lake in the night
in the teeth and hauled my stupid body
out of the storm into the trees

red osier dogwood stood onshore like a rope held out to me
I wore the skin off my palms
replaced my heart line with bark stains
I pulled myself into the bushes and cried

I'm not telling you this for pity
I didn't start this story to get you loving me
I'm just telling you why the side of the boat's busted in
and why I can't let anyone babysit
and why I still live here
I don't know

WIFE LIKE A PEBBLE

in the dusk his wife is like a pebble
she shines as if wet
wavering in a current
he watches her by firelight
wants to pin her down
lest she's so small a rock
she shifts and rolls away

when she works in the pines
she is a girl like a needle
sharp and flashing
she never looks at him in daylight
and it sticks in his flesh

in the tent she seems a cattail
when she stands to drop the clothes
from her body, all silk and lithe
he looks down at his hands
chapped from the weather
and wonders if she'll feather
when she ripens and drift away

WIFE/TRAPLINE

snow in the saddle two months early
when he wakes to september
she is gone

he sees her when his eyes are closed
he pictures her all winter
and gets no fur

she clears his traps before he gets there
he sees her
fingerprints in snow

SASQUATCH

scent of swamp and damp,
wafts from lank clumps of long fur
cleaving and tearing,
a lumbering walk, limp, walk:
the solitary brown traveller

~

hard scramble through blowdown
burrs
sweat matted brows
the long sweep of long arms
fending off horseflies,
the mosquito-plagued aimlessness

~

skunk cabbage, devil's club
rain and after rain:
rest and fistsful of morel
a stump for a view
of blackflies and mudflats,
black spruce, muskeg,
the muck-swallowed footprints
gone before the glance back

SUPPOSE THE POEM

suppose the words went back inside the pen
sucked up like spills
or thoughts you knew better than to release

suppose you wrote hoping
the words would take care of themselves
that they'd herd themselves like border collies
crossed with sheep – obedient even
as they raced ahead
wild with their own exuberance
suppose you wrote *exuberance*

suppose you never regret it
not even once
suppose you said it
and meant it

if the words come to you like supplicants
rubbing their blunt heads against your knees
and you stroke them calm
flattering them into order
then you meant it
and the poem was the form you were after   .

because wouldn't it be silly
to write something meaningless
something left-hand-margin heavy
to hold some thought you found ugly and abhorrent
until you supposed it lovely

vet's daughter

FOR FEAR OF FREEZING

yesterday the sheep were frozen in the field
alive inside cocoons of ice.
I could see their pupils moving.
today the cows do not low or swish their tails
they are silent.
I am afraid to look closely.

today I could believe that it will never thaw.
the snow doesn't crunch underfoot, it shatters.
each day is longer, more brittle than the last.
I can't hope for respite
when the cold is this ferocious.
I can't hope,
the days are wind-chapped and cracked.

tomorrow the crust on the snow
will thicken and sharpen.
the wind will whip at the fields
and the children will not leave the houses.
I clench my teeth, but I can't cry
here – you learn not to
come february
for fear of freezing.

CREMATORIUM

in plastic bags on tuesday nights
we load frozen corpses
from industrial-sized freezers
into the back of the suzuki.
we drive the kilometre fast
on the icy highway from the clinic to the mill
and in the compound, we dodge trucks and loaders
and stop at the base of the beehive burner.

chips of fire blast from the grill at the tip
hot orange flares in the noisy dark;
we haul stiff dogs and half-calves
up the metal stairs onto the clanging conveyor
that rattles dead cats to the top
and rolls them into the blaze.

dad yells up *these beasts are killing me*
and his faint voice jogs with every clanking step.
I can see fur through this white bag
still trying to pretend I hold only garbage;
I carry the little ones, birds and guinea pigs and gophers
while dad wrestles the doberman
and the stiff-limbed german shepherd
onto the belt that will jerk them into the flames.

bang-clink sings the chain that pulls
the chips up and up
and rolls the frozen animals
into a caged and giant fire
that whooshes and rails away the winter.

BOOTS

after whatever operation, whatever struggle
in the dust or dark in the yard by the trucks
he washes his bucket with a wide-bristled brush.
the loud complaint of stiff plastic on stainless steel
fills the barnyard.

he washes the inside with the water in the bucket,
he washes the outside by slopping vigorously,
he washes his hands and arms in the cooled water,
now red with blood and viscous with amniotic fluid.

he washes his boots at the end,
pours the last half-litre on to his feet
placed together so the water washes both of them;
green rubber emerges from the muck.
the steam rises.

he smiles to make lighter the night of a long ordeal
he looks kindly at you
through blood
dried to the lenses of his glasses.

VET'S DAUGHTER

kneeling in the sawdust and shit of a barnyard
the hot bulk of a downed stud horse beneath her
she holds a cock for the first time ever
the horse struggles and heaves
squeals into the dark
for help or mercy
while her father stitches its sheath
cut into two on a straight wire fence
she leans on the horse's back
feeling the sweat soak through her shirt
blood seeps around her fingers
she closes her eyes
and hangs on

NEW THEATRE

in the new theatre the heart monitor beeps,
your comfortable shoes scuff quietly on the floor.
that thing with the inflating black bag doesn't whoosh
in the corner like I remember it,
when the four of us kids stood on stools, no surgical caps,
breathing all over the inner flesh of a sleeping terrier
while we watched you work and tried not to handle
the perfect silver implements of surgery.

when you lost the tips of those two fingers in the snow-blower
it slowed you down; your spays and neuters
took twenty minutes instead of thirteen,
but you've trained your shorter fingers,
you are quicker now.

late at night you stand under the new lights in the new theatre
listening to cbc 2, clicking down one clamp to pick up another –
no kids in the audience, no audience,
but swift precision, same as ever.
maybe you miss the amplified breathing
of the dogs on your table, though the new machines
are more accurate. maybe you miss the clang of the kennels
as your kids locked each other in and screamed to be let out.

deep down, perhaps you don't. fast and efficient is your motto –
you embody it, in your blue cap, your white gown,
you don't falter when you pick up the scissors clamp
already off its hook and waiting on surgical paper
between the dog's outstretched legs. you never falter,
but do you notice the small space between the ends
of those two fingers and the dusty tips of your surgical gloves?

SLEEVES

spread like a starburst from the armpit seam
to his waist and outward: green, brown, red and wet
the found art of natural emissions
imbedded in the cotton of his short-sleeved dress shirt

up close the smell of animal almost overpowers us
when we hug, his sleeve leaves prints on my sleeve
of the work he's done already this morning while I slept
and the frost crystallized on the branches
and the moon stained the melting barnyard snow

YOU PAY MORE FOR A FARMCALL THAN YOU DO TO BRING IT IN

evening swallows dive from the lilac at the cats
a week-old calf lies spread legged
in the bed of a pickup truck
both slick with green poop

scours? the farmer asks
maybe, says dad
he slices the skin away from the muscle
through shitty brown fur
whitish fat

the calf's insides drip through the gap
between the tail-gate and the truck
what's the pasture like? dad asks
green, says the farmer
holding a hoof at shoulder height

most likely scours, says dad
thought so, says the farmer
he lays down the leg so the calf closes
he looks at my dad
my dad looks back
they did this last year, too

it costs more for the vet to get rid of the calf
than it does for the farmer to take him home
they bang up the tailgate and shake hands
the calf's eyes are closed
so the flies walk between its eyelashes
the swallows hunt the cats without mercy

NOT OLD ENOUGH TO DRIVE, BUT

just tall enough to hold
with every sinew of strength
a heifer's prolapsed uterus
though shaking with it, though struggling
not to let it slip further down
to knock against her hocks

you're not old enough to drive
but you're old enough to help
farmers ask if you'll be a vet
not bloody likely you say
and they laugh

these are the things you carry:
the calf-puller yoke, the pole and crank
or the bucket and brush and a jug full of water
or the case, two-handed
and it bangs against your knees

these are the things they notice:
you have no cow sense,
you have to decide whether
to climb the fence or crawl through,
the way you lean into your dad
when he's talking

you're big enough
to keep the electro-ejaculator
jammed in the rear of a bull
and you're loud enough
to scare cattle into a chute if you try,
but you're not his assistant
you're his kid.

afterward, when you're both
filthy and reeking
if there's light enough
he'll start to teach you to drive

agate hunters

at angles to the trans-country highway – ugly in spring, dusty
in summer with long winters, but under a migratory bird route
– the small-town hospital sits like a succulent above the river, fat
with life and death and make-do, small-town people succumbing
to cancerous tumours, colo-rectal disorders, lung collapses and
the handful of stab wounds and broken-bottle inflicted cuts that
make the story believable and leavable, and that's the point here
– the view, the stretch of the river, the goat-grazed islands in its
lowdown middle, the river meandering back and lazy forth, its
sandbars showing, the river brings you back

small-town girl gives birth to a small town baby girl below the
birds, above the river, to the tune of throngs of grand-voiced
geese giving wing, rising like one body above the rattly, rundown
nechako, shitting grandeur down like so much gorgeous refuse
– one baby rooming in in the room I roomed in with my mother
in the hospital my great-grandfather founded, finds herself blue-
eyes-wide to the world, to the sound of goose exodus, or its
preamble, the meet-and-greet before the departure south, away
from the small town, the river, away from the high-sky blue days
of early september in the year of her birth

small-town girl grow, then come home when it moves you, move
with the current and come back by the way of that feeling in your
arm when you sleep on it, follow the voices in your head, that
goodbye goose goodbye song, the pull of the river in september,
its scaly rib cage showing, breathe deep that full feeling of push
and pull the salmon feel spawning, throwing their used bodies
upstream against the current – small girl, blue-eyed and born
in the north, there's no escaping the feeling of freedom coming
upriver home, rock over rock, wind current, whorl, small town
or not, the river moves you

too deep a smell of black dirt and it's easter in vanderhoof, the front fields flooded hip-deep in meltwater –

all four of us pushed and dragged the rowboat over the dry patches and into the wet –

each sick to puking with need for tearing around outside so that hard labour hauling the boat from the driveway to the field left us sweaty, happy, unusually working together –

one wore hip waders, two had the peeling oars for poling and pushing off hummocks and clumps, davy was too small to do much but holler orders or say, *hoist the jolly roger, you faggots* –

the sun always shone on easter –

fuelled by chocolate and desire we were green inside and snapping, sailing furiously, wading furiously, whacking baby spruce trees to hell and landing *ho!* on small rises, we were four –

sucking in the almost-end of winter, in the fallow field, fishing uselessly with lego on a string –

NINE TIMES OUT OF TEN

in the field the geese sleep
with their necks bent artfully
down across their backs,
their heads under their wings.

away from the house
the light the town casts up makes our shadows long,
our arms impossible. you say, *there are geese out here –*
I'm going to get one, and I believe you
when you mime scooping and grabbing.

when I stumble I can't see the ground between the furrows.
birds rise like black sheets
against black earth and black sky.
you genuflect to the crop
and I am speechless in the noise
a thousand wings make slapping against a night.

nine times out of ten
when I imagine us I'm on my knees,
then you're on your knees, and we're those two kids
crying for lost chances, clutching an idea to our chests
and loving it though it beats us senseless.

walking back our shadows trail us.
they rise and shift when we step
like so many dark birds scared into flight,
behind and above us,
real for one second and then gone.

SOFT GEOGRAPHY

skin and air intermingle
each so near to the other
there is no space
between thought and water
regret and growth –
each tree ring
each shucked husk
of stonefly larva
in the swamp beside the road

the hollow inside is visible
in the clearcut across the highway
in the laughably spindly trees left –
the homeless woodpeckers
the heartless ache

on the roadside
the brush and scent of hay
the whiff of clover
age and wind fly off me
the inside seeps out

if here is the centre
of my own geography
and I am the remembrance
of yours – how is it
we are so far from ourselves?
we are so close
we are almost attached

THE AGATE HUNTERS

knee-deep in the wide bend before the bridge
with shorts rucked up their thighs
they stand against the flow, slowly ranging
back and forth across submerged gravel bars, grazing for agates

the cool of the river creeps into their skin
and the sun sinks behind goat island
certain slants of light allow the crystal
in the water to glint a beacon for a hand
they reach through current, not lapsing their gaze
though the water pulls it downstream

to pluck treasure from the ordinary, they are hopeful,
intent on a lucky find despite the miles of gravel muddied up
        with algae
they know the universe inside a rock held up to the evening sun
they know the well translucence is
drawing the eye deep inside the agate

the length of summer stretches across the broad sky
        and time is slowed
to a stop, like waves of colour captured mid-break

pockets full of paperweights they trail behind the tallest one
slow against the shallow current, now silhouettes in the water
below the slow bend of the river near the bird sanctuary
they count as they walk, rock by rock
their chill fingers muffle the rattling agates
the fortune in their pockets
the hope they cradle in hand

FIVE RIVERS: UNDER BRIDGES

1. nechako
a fish spine crusted to shore
scales sparkle
like lost things stuck to stone
the river trickles
slow

the nechako underfull,
but imagine it teaming with current:
ripped willows crammed to shore
logs jammed against bridge uprights
and placid massive white sturgeon
languid on the river bottom
unruffled by the water at full bore

undammed

man oh man
I wanna see that one

2. chilako
one bend available
bridged, seen at a whiz-pass
reeds at river's edge
eddy river right

despite the signs the kids park
and plunge
to the chicken farm river mud

chilako chilako
a song at high speed
the view in the rearview
makes you back up

3. nation
big, slow, sloping water
sweeps the swimming hole
hopefully full of eatin' fish
more likely fallen cars
from the nation river bridge

4. fraser (fort george)
meet the clang and stink of the black train bridge
dripping the rain into the broad brown river
can trees be proud?
the cottonwood aren't quitters
they draw the river up their roots
reach high toward sky
travellers in metal cars untouched
by river life, rife and humming
down below

5. stuart
two types of water swirl together
in a kindergarten picture of confluence:
silt and summer
the sweat of one long lake
giving up to smaller water
pressured into flow
from cloud to this: brown
and bright green

CANYON HOME

you work hard to attain hope
every day climbing out of the canyon bottom
like a pilgrim to your prayer flags
at the willowed edge
of the rock that rims your small house in

deep down the cold creek breaks off more
and more of the canyon floor
wearing it and your home ground
away from the sky
and the surface of thought

you climb because your mind depends on it
from willow bracken to bright mountain view
your climb defines the morning
the afternoon, the evening of your brain at peace
or warring

when the weather rushes in
your safe house holds you in stasis and you rail
for climbing, for the burn in your thighs and lungs
for the great small gain of getting up and out
of the deep home you have made among the fossils
and dirt and the homestead you keep
steady with your mind

THANKSGIVING

beside the dock I watch him
casting for casting's sake
his stepsister shakes her hair off her shoulders
it's early october and she's casting for casting's sake
I love her lipstick, how it never fades

the carp rise and fall and the trout are shore-spawning
all of it purposeless and lazy:
the trout, the talk about fishing for nothing
all this flirting with autumn

I love october and I love the stretch and pull
of his arm and his fly rod across the sky
out over the harmless blue lake
fish the size of thanksgiving dinner rise
up to him to see him
I swear they wink
then slowly swim away

he wants to catch the fish, he's so patient and pure – he ties his own flies, then tries them even when spoons are working. he helps me. he makes me a fish bonker out of a root. he scoops my fish out of the water, lays it down flapping, and smashes its head in.

I always catch the fish because I try so hard not to. he sets it all up – pulls the boat down the rocks, fills the gas tank, runs the motor, brings the smokes. he ties the lure on and throws it out of the boat. I read and catch fish that knock my book off my lap and put my cigarette out in the bloody slosh round my feet when I stand up to reel them in.

onshore he nails the burbot through the skull to a board in order to peel it, but when he peels it, it wiggles. we both jump back. when I start to cry he gives up, loosens the needle-nose pliers from the skin and we go down to the boat. marriage should always be like this – a motoring away together from horror to open water.

fishing after breakup, after that second false start into summer, the sun soaks into the backs of our arms, the parts in our hair and burns our noses. we hunker down, sheltered from the wind by the lifejackets we bought ourselves last christmas. we stare and reel, stare and reel. is this what you'd call a mackerel sky? yep. love, I've got one on.

BED POEM

when we talk small in the night eye to mouth, face to face, we recall the little moments of the days our children were born and first howling in the air, we talk soft and small, laughing small and smaller, smiling, looking eye to eye, then eyes to ceiling, then shut eyes, then dreams

when we talk big during daylight hours we don't converse we talk

in the bed we are children giggling together, our private life a real life that exists in the breath passed between us, our small rememberings are soap bubbles rising to the star decals on the ceiling before I fix the blankets and the conversation stops

in the day we are adult, separate, apart

late these days we lie together, foot to foot, and let the funny bits out, we create a confusion in the bed of covers and stories to sort out later, we laugh, get rowdy, get soft, sometimes cry, in the bed we say the names of our children, remember naming them, create them again with our words and breath

too late I apologize, then you apologize, then we fume, it is too bright or rainy to be honest, to say I made a mistake, I forgot, it gets late then later and all the things we don't say rise up in our throats blocking the laughter, this bill is overdue, the plants are thriving but dinner is poor comfort, I can't wait for bed, for foot to foot, eye to eye, for sleep

in the bed we are our children and our parents sorting out how the days work, how the parts of grownup life are not what we expected, we debrief with less complex words, we get out the hand cream and rub out mistakes, I am the orange you are peeling to feed me, you are the orange that nourishes us – *I'm so thirsty, let me bring you tea, I love you and the children, the kids are doing me in but they're so funny, you crack me up, come here and say that, love, I'm so sorry and happy, me too, sorry, happy, turn out the light*

THE LONG WAY
prince george

1
I drive the long way so I have a chance at a view
of the mills piled up like sweepers where the rivers meet
of the hills sculpted by said rivers into cutbanks
farther down the famous river

tack on ten more miles of radio freedom while my kids sleep
harnessed in the back, while I look and listen,
copping a peek at the herded-up wilderness
at bay behind the highway berms

earning two dollars extra canadian tire money next time I fill up
I drive the wrong way to the suburbs, up the hill
and breathe deep, look shallow
so I don't put ripples on the picture

2
I drive the long way home for the view and the opportunity
to turn off reality for a minute

I drive with a dirty desire for the woods unscathed
the road ungravelled
the ungulates piling up like foam on a high creek

3
what did I expect, moving back to a northern town?
to raise my kids to adulthood without the bite marks of cougars
in their limbs or on their psyches?
to get some cultural job that saves the arts,
artists, trees, and paper?
to enjoy ingesting the airborne wastes of three mills?

while wasting fossil fuels I gaze at the hinterland
with winter coming on and chores back in college heights
I brake, coming home, and jump the bump in the highway
to coast the last crumbs of soaring
to find the crows in my bear-tipped garbage can
the kids asleep in the back
the credits rolling on my short escape
from home to home

LOVE IS A VAST GEOGRAPHY
princeton

bing cherries ripe to bursting
make me take you
in my mouth
it's the sagebrush
the lake mouth
this swimming in landscape
love is a vast geography
and I'm trying to eat my way out

~

I don't mean I don't love you but also this:
chafed old orchards
stunted apple trees
the bare spots between them

~

love is a vast geography
and making it is crazy – the valley
running out of room
eventually butting up to the tulameen
close my eyes and I'm in it – you
the rapid mid-river
the current roughing me up
head downriver, then surfacing, gasping
the pillows off the end of the bed

~

love is vast and I'm ranging
section to section
indian land and crown land
dry grass and tree hollow

roll over and let me forage

~

where ticks wait in the long grass
where if you walked I'd ride you and gorge
on what you're made of:

the slow start of the creek
it's trickling finish
the wild stuff in the middle
the great long land of you
the way I've yet
to explore you fully

~

love is a vast geography, sweetheart
and here's to artful
continuous and constant
mapping

Understand love is a vast geography
–Charles Lillard

fall and burn

1
the chalk taste of ashes
the burns in your wool pants
the hours without (me, the baby)
the hrumm of skidoo, the heat
and shifty weight under you

you drive for hours around a lake
because bc has no shortcuts
while this pine-beetle plague
has been recognized by none

but the fallers know the truth: the futility
the heat of fall and burn piles left untended

2
barny plowed his sled into a hollow
and then a tree, then he busted it proper
and had to double for a week before he fixed it

and it was almost funny –
how he drove it like a bastard
gunning for jumps in thick stands of pine
pine with no signs of affliction, yet
just runny sores

and you were pissed that he took it so lightly
then learned he took it so heavy he longed
for the split of his helmet-less head
on some punkin in the deep wood
no regard for you (or me, or the baby)

3
we owed nothing:
we bought a skidoo, new tires
a chainsaw and a highchair
with no pause, no credit card
no idea at what point on the map
of our lives we were pinned
spinning, on the edge of a lake
in northern canada –
a place we'd lucked into
by birth and happenstance

you grew a beard,
you got creases around your eyes
I read, nursed the baby
spent too much time at the window –
the winter, in early black
graced our table
and we laughed, played risk
felled all sorts of things
with great sharp shiny chains
and our bare senseless hands

4
alone from dark to dark
and when the light lifted, a whiteout:
frozen lake, sky, no difference

night fell black
and no answers
just me (the house, the baby)

waiting at the window
staring at myself reflected
I wished you home, wished us on

in the hours and hours while you returned
unpegged and out of range, but orbiting
us, the lake, (the sleeping baby)

5
what happened to the next new family of three
riding (man, woman, baby in the pack)
on a snowmobile across a lake
for no other reason than movement?

we built a man-sized snowman on the sled-track
invisible in the falling snow
maybe as testament to our having been there
or as a booby trap – death lurking silently
in smooth balls of stacked snow

maybe pending doom is eroded by the wind and weather
softened with time and melted by the sun
like change creeps up on us, red pine by red pine:
we don't notice a difference until we can't see
healthy green needles for the miles and miles
of sloughed bark, blackened pitch holes
the standing dead, looming all around us

6
fall and burn piles bigger than the house
built bucked log by bucked log and blazing

I picture the two of you, motors ticking
saws in hand, leaving the fires burning

because nothing can stop this oncoming wave of red
not heat, not falling trees, not pheromones

not one thing pegs you at a fire edge
with your friend who's since gone south

not one thing except a locust cloud,
except me: my desire, myself reflected

ACKNOWLEDGEMENTS

Earlier versions of some of these poems have appeared in *CV2*, *filling Station*, the *Inner Harbour Review*, *Northwords*, *Prism* and *Westword*. Some poems were included in chapbooks: *here you learn not to* published by Smoking Lung Press, and *home when it moves you* published by Creekstone Press. My thanks to the editors of each.

I had many helpful readers in my journey toward a book: Ariel Gordon, Robert Hilles, Donna Kane, Sheila Peters, Al Rempel, Laisha Rosnau, Travis Sillence, George Sipos, Fred Stenson, Anna Swanson, Betsy Trumpener, Sue Wheeler, Judy Wigmore and Silas White. I'm greatly indebted to them for their comments and encouragements.

For camaraderie and support, I would like to thank the many writers working out of Prince George and generally north of Hope, especially the Candlefish Writers of Destiny (past members included). I'm grateful to have attended the Banff Centre for the Arts, and for the writers I met there. Thanks to George Sipos for suggesting I apply and for nudging me until I did. For kinship and friendship, I am grateful to my cousin Fabienne Calvert Filteau. I'm indebted to Derk Wynand for being direct, always, and for advice that continues to resonate.

Once again, thank you to the communities of Vanderhoof, Fort St. James and Prince George for inspiration and for safe harbour.

Some of these poems are for Jamie, Susie and David, who shared in my charmed childhood, and for my parents, Walter and Judy Wigmore, whom I thank especially for the books and the freedom. Thank you to Elly, Emmett and Travis Sillence, every day, for equal amounts love and craziness.

This book is for Jennifer Robyn Goff. For the girls we were and for the woman she would have become.

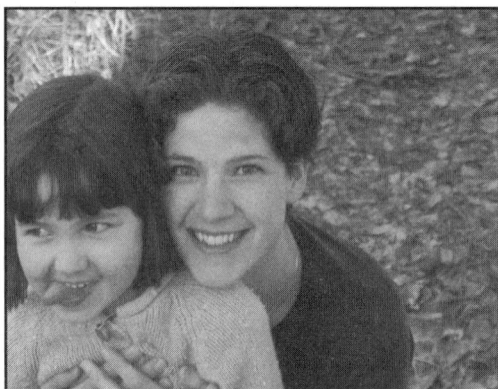

Gillian Wigmore grew up in Vanderhoof, BC, graduated from the University of Victoria in 1999, and currently lives in Prince George. She has been published in *Geist*, *CV2*, *filling Station* and the *Inner Harbour Review*, among others. Her first chapbook, *home when it moves you*, was published by Creekstone Press in 2005.